UNDERSTANDING AFFILIATE MARKETING

AN INTERNET MARKETING GUIDE ON HOW TO MAKE MONEY ONLINE THROUGH PRODUCTS, WEBSITES AND SERVICES

BY SMART READS

Visit:
www.smartreads.co/freebooks
to receive Smart Reads books for FREE

Check us out on Instagram:
www.instagram.com/smart_readers
@smart_readers

ABOUT SMARTREADS

Choose Smart Reads and get smart every time. Smart Reads sorts through all the best content and condenses the most helpful information into easily digestible chunks.

We design our books to be short, easy to read and highly informative. Leaving you with maximum understanding in the least amount of time.

Smart Reads aims to accelerate the spread of quality information so we've taken the copyright off everything we publish and donate our material directly to the public domain. You can read our uncopyright below.

We also believe in paying it forward and donate 5% of our net sales to Pencils of Promise to build schools, train teachers and support child education.

As a thank you for being a Smart Reader you can choose 3 FREE audiobooks from audible.com. Simply sign up for free by visiting www.audibletrial.com/Travis to get your first book.

After you sign up email me at Hello@SmartReads.co and tell me what other 2 books on audible you want and I will send you 2 Free Credits to download the books of your choice.

Thanks for choosing Smart Reads.
Sincerely,

Travis & the Smart Reads Team

TABLE OF CONTENTS

INTRODUCTION

There were many success stories in mainstream culture throughout the nineties. Jim Carrey went from being a small-time stand-up comedian on the toilet scene to one of Hollywood's most bankable stars, while a bunch of unassuming hairy young men from Seattle recorded an album in LA and became the defining band of a decade. Their name? Nirvana.

But the thing that had the most lasting effect and influence in the nineties was the world wide web, which reached everyone on the planet and changed our lives forever, including the way we shop, watch movies and work. The Internet is as big now as it was then, and will only get even bigger. Unlike a band or a movie star, it isn't going to slow down and disappear. Age will not faze it.

Soon after its explosion, companies realized that the Internet represented a new and amazing marketing platform. The opportunity to expand a company's consumer base was evident, and once search engines were invented, there was all of a sudden a new way for a business to get their products seen by millions of people around the globe. Amazon wouldn't be selling books to the locals - it would be selling them to everyone.

After some time, affiliate marketing was born.

The goal of this book is to track the history of this particular type of marketing, defining what it is and how it operates, before examining the pros and cons. By the end, you will be armed with the skill that will help you take advantage of affiliate marketing, either as a merchant or as an affiliate.

CHAPTER 1: UNDERSTANDING AFFILIATE MARKETING

If you've already looked into Internet marketing, you've probably already come across the term "affiliate marketing." But what is it exactly?

Affiliate marketing is essentially a form of pay-for-performance advertising. Essentially, it's advertising that is based on performance. The purchase will pay its advertiser money only when it can see the ad campaigns results.

It's a form of advertising that is getting more and more popular, largely thanks to the explosion of the Internet. Tools like Google Analytics lets us measure how well (or how badly) our users are responding to ads.

A company will hire at least one affiliate, but often they will hire more. The affiliate then works on the company's marketing on the Internet, and are paid according to how many visitors or consumers their marketing efforts bring in.

In simple terms, you are promoting a businesses product, website or service and are rewarded according to your marketing campaigns' performance.

There are 4 players which affiliate marketing works through:

- Merchant – essentially, the retailer, or brand
- Network - contains any offers from which the affiliate can pick from
- Affiliate(s) - known also as publishers
- Customers

Affiliate marketing has expanded over the years, and is now more complicated than ever. As such, more players have been drafted in, including affiliate marketing teams and even so-called super affiliates.

Affiliate marketing is sometimes mistakenly used interchangeably with referral marketing, but this is erroneous. It's a common mistake, and is often made because both forms of marketing rely on 3rd parties to try and gain more customers. The difference though is that financial motivations are the primary driver behind affiliate marketing techniques and subsequent sales.

Affiliate marketing is certainly not the most popular type of marketing. It's one the advertisers often overlook in favor of other strategies. For example, website syndication and SEO are more popular.

With that said, a number of e-retailers who use affiliate marketing considers it to be a key part of their overall strategy.

CHAPTER 2: A BRIEF HISTORY LESSON

Origins

Paying commissions or revenue sharing for businesses that are referred is a fairly old concept, and predates the Internet. The concept first found its way online at the end of 1994, around 4 years after the Internet had begun to take off.

Affiliate marketing as an online concept was developed by William J. Tobin, who went on to patent it. His business was called PC Flowers and Gifts, and operated on a network called Prodigy from 1989 until 1996. Halfway through, its sales amount were beyond $6,000,000 a year, and in 1998 the company came up with a business model that allowed them to pay a commission of the sales to Prodigy.

Together with IBM, which had shared ownership of Prodigy, William J. Tobin launched a beta version of his business in 1994. In 1995, he released a commercial version. At this moment, they had around 2,600 affiliate marketing partners online.

Tobin knew that his business model had immense value, and wrote of applications for affiliate marketing at the start of 1996. He received a U.S. patent number, as well as a Japanese patent number.

One of the earliest innovators in affiliate marketing was a company called CyberErotica. This company utilizes a cost-per-click program.

In 1994 came another innovation. CD-NOW launched a BuyWeb program late in the year, with the idea being that any music-based websites should review or list any albums they thought their site visitors would be interested in.

The website would then offer the visitor a link to CD-NOW, where they would be able to buy the album. The idea blossomed after a series of conversations with music label Geffen Records, who wanted to sell their albums on their actual website. Not wanting to develop the feature by themselves, they got CD-NOW on board, who would look after the orders. CD-NOW was then able to link a prospective customer from a band's website to Geffen's website.

In the summer of 1996, an associate program was started by Amazon, which would allow associates the chance to place banners or text links for books on their own site. Also, they were able to link to the Amazon home page directly. Whenever a visitor to the associates site went on to Amazon and actually purchased a book, the associate would receive a commission

Amazon was not the first organization to offer such an incentive, but theirs was the first one that truly caught on.

Historic Development

Since its beginnings, affiliate marketing has rocketed. When they were first conceived and launched, e-commerce websites weren't seen as anything above and being a gimmicky marketing tool that would partly boost sales. Over time, however, more and more businesses integrated them with their broader marketing strategies.

By 2006, affiliate networks had amassed total sales that exceeded £2,160,000,000 in the UK alone. Total sales around the world were $6,500,000,000 in U.S. dollars, with sources ranging from telecom to gambling to travel and retail.

It was the retail, adult entertainment and gambling sectors where affiliate marketing was proving to be the most popular, while the three sectors that have been forecast to grow more than any others were financial, travel and mobile phones. The gaming, service and entertainment sectors were not expected to be far behind.

Web 2.0

Web 2.0, which is largely defined by interactive services and communities, played a huge role in the rise of affiliate marketing, and indeed gave this form of marketing a proper platform, allowing for a better connection between affiliates and merchants.

Writers, bloggers and indie website owners were also able to take advantage of affiliate marketing in the era of Web 2.0. For example, publishers who found it hard to get traffic are able to place affiliate ads via contextual ads on websites.

New forms of media have changed the looks of ads. YouTube, for example, has a rule, which stipulates that its video makers must embed ads via the affiliate network which Google runs. The more unethical affiliates have therefore found it hard to make as much cash, and this is down to the advancements, which are able to identify fraudulent affiliates.

CHAPTER 3: LAUNCHING A BUSINESS

Now that the history is out of the way, let's take a look at what you need to do to launch your very own affiliate marketing business.

Via affiliate marketing, you can make commissions by selling another company's products or services. The best thing? You don't even need to leave your own home!

The second best thing is that becoming an affiliate is actually really easy. Firstly, it's important you sell what you know. Sticking to a niche that you understand is key, especially when you're first starting out. Find a niche that is either something you're passionate about, or something you're already involved with for a living. If your passion is books and not fishing, it makes a whole lot of sense to center your efforts on books. Otherwise, you're probably going to waste a lot of time.

Secondly, you need to launch a website which is related to your niche. A website is very important. Without one, you can't be an affiliate. In fact, the first thing a company is going to ask you is what your website is all about. It has to be relevant to their niche, and it needs to look presentable and engaging. Otherwise, they're not going to be interested. You don't need to spend an absolute fortune on a website, nor do you need to employ a professional web designer. WordPress has free versions, and they walk you through the whole process.

Thirdly, you should take some time to research a few affiliate programs.

Don't find an affiliate program and immediately decide that's the one you want. What if it isn't relevant to what you're planning to sell? What if there are betters ones? Amazon is the most popular affiliate program because it sells practically anything you can think of. It's a good place to make your debut. ClickBank is another good one that is popular because the company offers super good commissions.

Fourthly, you need to sign up to an affiliate program. This won't cost you any money, and you should definitely be on your guard if the program asks for credit card details. This should not happen, and if it does it's most likely to be a scam. Businesses will, however, request your bank account or PayPal info. Don't worry - they need this info in order to pay out your commissions!

Fifthly, you need to add affiliate links to your content. You won't want to come across as too salesy to your site visitors, as it can put them off returning. The best way to strike up a rapport with your visitors while making a sale is to write great content relevant to the niche, before slipping in a link to the product somewhere inside the content.

Let's say you're promoting a hammock that is on sale on Amazon. You'd create a blog all about hammocks, and start writing articles such as "10 Reasons To Go Camping With A Hammock." Then, somewhere in the middle of the blog posts, you would include a link to the product on Amazon. It's important that your content is strong and engages the reader. You DON'T want it to look as though you're just throwing any old blog post together so as to make a sale. This is the part where you need to wear your best copy writing hat.

Sixthly, you should add visual ads to your sidebar. If your website has a sidebar (and it really should,) think about adding visual ads. It's easy to do this, and it's effective. An eye-catching visual ad will capture a visitor's attention and possibly compel them to click and make a purchase.

Seventhly, you need to keep producing good, relevant content. One or two great blog posts are okay for one or two days. But that's it. If you want people to keep returning to your site so that you can make more sales, you'll need to produce regular content that is good. Rubbish content will drive people away. Remember that content always was and always will be King.

Eighthly, you need a way of measuring your success - I recommend analytics tools. Analytics tell you how many items you have sold, which is kind of important as it helps you to track your progress. For example, if you weren't making any sales but didn't know it, you wouldn't make the necessary changes that could potentially bring in more sales. Google Analytics is my personal favorite. It gives you an in-depth access to your visitors' demographics, and doesn't cost any money to use. Other things to look out for are how many views your posts are getting, as this will tell you what needs tweaking and what's already working fine. Analytics is basically a helpful way of giving you an insight into what you need to double down on, and what you need to lose.

Ninthly, you will need to start preparing for taxes at some point. I know this sounds really boring, but it's smart that you cover your back. If you're getting a LOT of commissions, paying your fair share of tax is legal. It's something you have to do. It's classed as income, even if it isn't a conventional form of income. Any business you work with will send you a form called a 1099. But before they send it, make sure you inform the IRS of your income.

Tenthly, you will need to eventually look at ways of expanding your business. Your business will expand or it will contract. It won't do both, and this is why you need growth. Once your business begins to shrink, any returns will reduce.

For this reason, I recommend that you market more than a single product. Always keep an eye out for anything new that you could sell. Check other affiliate sites and see what they're offering. Keep abreast of new trends as well as new companies that are forming affiliate programs. They might have something for you.

To make sure your business expands, you should also promote it online as much as possible. Don't take a backseat here but be proactive. Make things happen. Get your business seen by people.

There are many ways you can promote your business. Social media and email are my two favorites, but you could also work with bloggers and write guest posts on their site. Be a bit creative with this one.

Eleventh, you should delegate tasks. Yes, you're an affiliate. But that doesn't mean that once you start raking in money, you shouldn't delegate. You totally should! Eventually, you won't have the time to do everything. So why not hire someone else to take care of the tedious tasks that you just don't fancy doing yourself? Yes, you will have to set aside a budget for this. But the benefits in the long run will be huge. Delegation always reaps rewards.

The twelfth thing you need to do is automate whatever can be automated. Do you use digital marketing tools already? Great. If not, it's time to start using them. Why? Because they will save you SO much time. Yes, they cost money. But like delegation, they will bring you a lot of rewards.

CHAPTER 4: HOW TO MAKE CASH AS AN AFFILIATE

Is affiliate marketing a get-rich-quick scheme where all you need to do is sell stuff online? Definitely not.

It's certainly possible to make money online via affiliate marketing and that's why we're here. However, because this proposition is so attractive, there are many people just like you who want to do what you want to do. This means competition.

Fierce competition.

To be a success, it's essential that you know the market, including what is needed, how products are promoted, and what works and what doesn't.

Don't Pick Too Many Products

A simple mistake is to enter various programs and choose loads of products to promote. Why is this a mistake? Because you are taking on too much, and cannot possibly master every single niche. You will become a jack of all trades yet a master of none. Pick a niche and double down on it. Don't try to do everything. It just won't work.

Promote Your Products On Numerous Sources of Traffic

You can display ads on your site, but this should not be the only place you place ads. The more traffic sources you use, the more commissions you'll get. It's basic math. You could use Google AdWords to help you out with this. Go to your AdWords account and create an ad, before placing in the ads target page URL and your affiliate link. These campaigns can get costly if you don't keep an eye on them, so it's important that you keep checking up. Otherwise, you'll find that you're spending more money on advertising than making money from your business.

Track, Measure and Test Your Campaign

How many strategies should you use to promote the products? Certainly more than one. You don't know which strategies will work and which won't until you try them out. Experiment and split test to work out how well a campaign is doing. If it's doing okay, you can tweak it. If it's doing terribly, you can ditch it altogether. Sometimes, all it takes is a few minor adjustments to see huge boosts in profit, but you won't know where these changes need to take place unless you track, measure and test your campaigns. You could also invest in conversion software that shouldn't cost too much money.

Find Out How In-Demand A Product Is

Before you commit to promoting a product, first make sure that there is a good demand for it. If there isn't, you're just not going to get anywhere. You might get a lot of site visitors, but if you haven't got what they want, you'll be left frustrated.

Stay Up-To-Date With Trends

Things are always changing in affiliate marketing and there is always a new method or technique being introduced. For this reason, I strongly suggest you stay on top of the latest trends as much as possible. You do not want to fall behind the competition simply because you didn't pay enough attention.

Pick Your Merchant Carefully

You're here to promote a product, but you're also here to promote a company. The last thing you want is for one of your site visitors to be unhappy with the company. It will reflect badly on you, and could damage your reputation. Check for a company's reputability and make sure they are worth working with.

Invest In Useful Tools

As long as you see yourself dedicating a lot of time to affiliate marketing, it's well worth investing in the proper tools that will make your workflow more efficient. For example, I strongly suggest adding the Affiliate Link Manager plugin if WordPress is powering your website.

CHAPTER 5: COMPENSATION TECHNIQUES

Most Common Compensation Techniques

The most popular compensation technique is the pay per sale, otherwise known as revenue sharing. It's used by up to 80% of affiliates. Cost by action, meanwhile, is used by around 19%. The remaining affiliate programs use cost per click.

Diminished Techniques of Compensation

Although cost per click isn't used all that much these days, display advertising and paid search do still rely on them a lot.

Cost per mile is another diminished compensation technique. All it needs is for an affiliate to publish an ad on their website and ensure that site visitors see it for them to get paid a commission. Pay per click requires a visitor to click on the ad before any money is paid out. Cost per click was in widespread use at the start of affiliate marketing, but isn't used as much today, primarily because businesses became savvy to click frauds. However, although established e-commerce and online advertising markets rarely use either CPM or CPC, emerging industries do.

For example, over in China, where affiliate marketing is different to what it is here in the West, a number of affiliates are paid a cost per day flat rate, while there exist plenty of networks, which offer CPC or CPM.

Affiliate/Performance Marketing

If a publisher is using CPM or CPC, they won't care if a site visitor is someone they actually want to attract. All that matters is they've earned a commission. As such, all burdens of risk lie squarely on the advertiser and not the publisher.

However, cost per action or cost per sale demands the affiliate to be more proactive because to get paid, you'd need a site visitor to first visit a website - and then buy something. Consequently, the affiliate must find ways of driving targeted traffic so that there is a better chance of more conversions. In this way, the affiliate is sharing the risk with the advertiser and they are working towards a common goal.

Performance marketing is another technique of compensation and it's a bit more traditional in the sales world. Whenever there is a conversion, the employees get a commission. There are often incentives added to encourage employees to exceed set targets. You can look at affiliates as part of a businesses sales team. It's not an entirely true statement, however, because an affiliate marketer cannot directly engage the customer once they enter the advertiser's website. They have to sit back and wait and see what happens. This is very different to a sales team who are always with the client, right up to the end.

A Multi-Tier Program

Some advertisers use a multi-tier program, in which commissions are spread out in a hierarchal referral network.

Essentially, Marketer 1 is an affiliate. They get a commission each time there is conversion. Let's say that Marketer 2 and 3 then sign up to this affiliate program and want in on the action. They use Marketer 1's sign-up code, which means that any conversions they make will also benefit Marketer 1, who will receive a small portion of the commission.

However, not many affiliate programs are multi-tier. Most are one-tier. One of the reasons for this is that they can often get too complicate and are seen as largely unnecessary.

CHAPTER 6: COMMON MISTAKES YOU NEED TO AVOID

More and more people are becoming affiliate marketers because it's so easy to sign up and payments are made fairly regularly. But to succeed, you need a strategy and you need to be consistent.

There are many mistakes that many new affiliate marketers can't seem to avoid but for the purposes of this book I'm going to focus on thirteen of them. Make a few of these (or even just one) and you will hinder your chances of growth.

Failing To Focus On The Pre-Offer

Too many affiliate marketers concentrate on the results and administrations of a customer, or they relay the positive and negative facets of administration of specific items to their potential clients. When an affiliate marketer does this, he is making a costly, time-consuming error. Your objective should be to pre-offer to the customer. Do NOT offer a product with an uncertain or unknown date of release to your potential clients.

Don't Promote Services And Products Unless You've Used Them

A big mistake is to promote services and products you haven't used. You might think that doing this is okay because it saves you time. But this is a big mistake that can ruin your long-term prospects. Clients prefer to buy items from sales reps that have the same item at home themselves. It inspires confidence in the product and trust in the sales rep.

As an affiliate marketer, you need to nurture similar levels of confidence and trust, and you can do this by promoting services and products that you have used - and enjoyed - yourself. Spend some time getting to know a product or service. It doesn't matter what it is or whether or not you wouldn't ordinarily buy such a thing. You need to get to know it.

Customers are less likely to convert if you clearly don't know what the product is about. They are looking to you to give them a bit of a guiding hand and, believe it or not, their next step is often dependent on what you have to say. Spend some time getting to know a product or service. It will be time well spent.

Working Without Email List

Do you need an email rundown to be a successful affiliate marketer? You bet. With an email list, you can share new products and services with clients time and time again. If you do not have an email list, you lose an invaluable opportunity to gain repeat customers and repeat commissions. It makes no sense not to have an email list and not doing so is a strategic faux pas.

Choosing The Wrong Program and Product

Look, there are a lot of affiliate programs out there, and not all of them will be the right ones of you.

Established affiliate marketers are very good at picking out the right ones and ignoring the wrong ones.

How do you know when a program is right for you? Normally, you would pick ones that sell products you know and have used (or will use), as well as ones, which have high commissions.

There are other things to consider too, though:

• Convenience
• Payout
• Regularity of items

You should also take into consideration how much time you'll need to dedicate to a program in order to have any success. The last thing you want to do is overstretch yourself by working on a program that is too demanding and where the rewards aren't proportionate to the amount of time you're spending on it.

Commission or payout is another thing you should look into closely. Find out how long it will take you to pre-offer a product or service and then adjust the commissions for each deal so it reflects how much time and effort you have devoted to a sale. Also, it's a good idea to sound out an affiliate program beforehand to the extent that you know how usable it is and how supportive it is of their clients. Communication and engagement between both parties is key, as it helps to build a rapport and instill motivation and enthusiasm.

Ask yourself if you could get enthusiastic about a product or service if the affiliate programs themselves weren't showing any enthusiasm? I doubt you could.

Failing To Commit

Once you have settled on an affiliate program which you know is right for you, it's then essential for you to commit to it 100%. To be a success at affiliate marketing, you need to be tolerant, patient, dedicated. And you need to take responsibility. Don't go blaming others when things aren't going right. Be a leader here and take responsibility.

If you're not the most organized person in the world, and if you tend to neglect certain things despite your initial enthusiasm, it's a good idea to create a schedule so that you always dedicate enough time to your affiliate marketing each week. Without dedication, you just won't succeed at this.

Promoting Too Many Products and Services

You might be of the belief that the more different types of stuff you sell, the more successful you'll be at this affiliate marketing game. Totally wrong. You have to ask yourself if you really have the time and energy to sell numerous items all at the same time. The likely answer is that you don't. The more work you try to do and the more niches you try to fill, the more you will fail. Expand deals - don't expand quantity.

Promoting Awful Products

Will people really buy anything? No. And if you do manage to convince them to buy any old junk, they'll return it and never visit your site again. Quality is what connects you to the customer. It makes them happy and creates a positive association of you in their mind.

If you decide to pursue poor items, the customers will soon guess. They're not stupid. And they'll avoid you. And let's say they do make a purchase - then what? They'll receive the product in the mail, realize it's awful, and you'll never see them again.

Moreover, when someone buys a piece of junk, it's just luck - bad luck for them and good luck for you. Is this how you want to operate? What you want to do as an affiliate marketer is establish trust between yourself and the customers. And you can only do this by offering them quality products and services. Link them to top quality products and you'll make sales. Even better, the same satisfied customers will come back to see what else you've got. They might also share your site with others.

Not Getting A Blog Or Website

You can't expect to become a rip-roaring success at this if you only promote via social media, mailing lists and paid ads. What you really need is your own blog or website.

Websites and blogs are the best ways to promote affiliated products and services. Using your professional name, you can create rapport with your site visitors. Blogs are friendly and personable ways of engaging the customer and convincing them, not only to make a purchase, but also to come again. Over time, you could easily build yourself an army of loyal consumers who use your site to help them make better buying decisions. You will also find that a blog or website saves you a lot of time.

Not Doing Any Keyword Research
If you've never done keyword research before, you'll need to start doing it soon. Without it, you won't be getting as much traffic as you could be getting.

Keyword research tells you exactly what customers are looking for. Once you know what they're tapping into Google, you can then start using those terms in your content so that you appear on the first page of Google. Bear in mind that SEO is a science and an art, and you need to dedicate a substantial amount of time and effort into getting it right. If it isn't something you are well versed in, you could hire someone to take care of this for you.

Not Including Good Reviews

If a customer is unsure about a product, they'll read customer reviews to get a better idea of whether it's something they should be buying or not. You can only tell them so much. Customer reviews help to fill in the gaps. And if lots of customers have bought and enjoyed the product, the buyer will become convinced that they will enjoy it too.

A good review should outline what is in it for the customer. What are the benefits. How will their life improve if they bought this product? What will it do for them? It should also go over the features while always bearing in mind what these features will do for them. If there are no reviews on your site, a potential buyer might check another site. A review is often what convinces them to make the click.

Failing To Believe In Yourself

Do you believe you can succeed as an affiliate marketer? Because if you don't believe, you won't succeed. Anyone who enters a new venture probably has some trepidation. But what separates the winners from the losers is mindset. In other words, winners believe they can do this. Losers do not.

Success is not entirely built on belief, but belief is your foundation from which everything else grows, including the ability to take action. Only when you have enough belief in yourself to succeed at affiliate marketing can you begin and only when you have enough knowledge can you have enough belief. Learn first, then you can start to believe.

Believing You Will Become Rich Quickly

Is this a get-rich-quick scheme? Absolutely not. Affiliate marketing is just another method of making cash. If you are here to make a load of money in a short period of time before trying something else, you're entering the wrong game. You need to pay a lot of attention to be successful at affiliate marketing and need to have resolve and patience if things are going slowly at first. All the successful people in business have long-term goals. They don't get carried away with short-term glories.

CHAPTER 7: THE BENEFITS OF AFFILIATE MARKETING

Affiliate marketing is an inexpensive marketing strategy - in fact it's the cheapest relative to how much you can make from it. It has both advantages and disadvantages, but for the purpose of this chapter we're going to take a look at the benefits of affiliate marketing.

You Can Sell A Product Directly

As an affiliate marketer, you don't need to spend any time creating a product. All you need to do is begin selling.

For you, it's as easy as choosing a service or product, before finding a way of generating sales and leads so that you and the business you're working with turn a profit. Basically, once you get the links, it's time to start selling right away. You don't need to worry about shipping, costs, or anything else.

You Can Focus On Just A Single Area

Your business is the hyperlinks. That's it. They are your specialist area. You don't need to concern yourself with anything else! Do you need to worry about the money transactions? Totally not! That's none of your concern, and you should be happy that it isn't! All you're here to do is promote the product or service and bring in lots of leads. Oh, and you can also care about the money you're going to make.

You Don't Need To Invest Much Money

If you're new to affiliate marketing and don't have a lot of money behind you, the good news is that it doesn't matter. This isn't like a business, which requires you to have capital. You don't need to take out a loan or attract investors. All you need are a few tools, many of which are free to download and use.

You Get To Learn About New Marketing Worlds

Before you begin working as an affiliate marketer, it's important that you pick a market that is related to the services and products you'll be selling.

You could look at other marketers for inspiration. For example, perhaps you know a marketer who is making lots of cash selling kitchen products. Check out his strategy and see what you can learn from it. Then, use what you've learned, take it onboard and base part of your campaign around it. This is called modeling and everyone does it. It's a lot quicker to learn from other peoples' mistakes than your own!

You Get To Earn Money!

Okay, this is why you're reading this book in the first place - you want to earn money. Once you have perfected your affiliate marketing method, you are ready to reap the rewards.

You can use any number of conventional marketing strategies, such as content marketing or SEO to promote your service or product. Once you've placed your hyperlinks online, the next step is to wait for an email that will tell you how much cash you are making. A creative affiliate marketer makes money eventually. They always do. You don't need to stress yourself if things don't fall into place straight away. The money will come. As long as you have a drive for this, you really can't go wrong.

You benefit from affiliate marketing and so does the brand. Here are a few ways in which the brand themselves benefit from affiliate marketing:

They Get More Leads Quicker

Companies who use affiliate marketing as part of their wider marketing strategy generates more leads and sales. It's simple mathematics - the more marketing campaigns you have, the more traffic you'll have, the more leads you'll have, the more sales you'll enjoy. Affiliate marketing, then, is certainly not just benefiting you.

They Earn Through Delegating

For businesses that are savvy about delegation, affiliate marketers are great because they take care of one of the toughest parts of the sales process - promoting the product so that they edge out rivals. While the affiliate marketer is busy taking care of promoting a product or service, the business doesn't need to put too much time and effort of their own into doing the same thing. They can instead focus on other core aspects of their organization.

They Get Increased Market Share Without Putting In Any Extra Effort

A business needs to be very careful about choosing an affiliate marketer. They can't just select any old affiliate marketer and expect it to work out for them. They need to pick one who they know is going to maximize profits.

There are therefore a few things the business will look for in an affiliate marketer, such as whether or not they have their own website and how much they know about the businesses brand and niche.

Picking the right affiliate marketer increases the businesses market share and the only extra effort they need to put in is when it comes to choosing who should promote their products.

CHAPTER 8: DISADVANTAGES

Just as there are benefits to affiliate marketing, there are also downsides. Before a business throws themselves into an affiliate marketing adventure, it's good to know what the pitfalls are, as well as any reasons why you might decide not to do this.

Affiliates Pop Up All The Time

Once you launch yourself on the Internet as an affiliate marketer, you might find that everything is going super swimmingly at first. You're getting plenty of traffic and conversions and making a stack of cash.

But then, look out - there is another affiliate marketer in town and they're taking all your visitors! This happens. New affiliates spring up all the time. You just have to hold your nerve, and maybe tweak what you are doing. The main thing is not to get disheartened.

Your Bottom Line Will Be Faded By Network And Affiliate Commissions

Affiliates improve sales. But with more sales can come more costs. The commissions that a business may pay out to an affiliate range between 5-10%. If a business is also part of a wider affiliate network, there will be even more costs to pay out.

Profits Can Actually Go Down

Perhaps the biggest drawback to affiliate marketing is that profits can actually go down by working with affiliates. Consider this: A business has just launched and is selling quite well. Eventually, they decide to get a few affiliates on board to increase sales. As it happens, the sales do go up.

Trouble is, aggregate sales are pretty much the same. How come? This is often because an affiliate used an affiliate code to convince a potential buyer to visit your website. Therefore, it's time for you to make a payout to the affiliate. There are many reasons for this, from fake promos to SEO techniques. Some will even use fake coupons. Some crafty affiliates even use a trick whereby pretty much every visitor to your website is coming through them.

An Affiliate May Not Have Much Respect For Your Brand

Of course you want your affiliates to respect your brand as much as you do. After all, you've dedicated a lot of time, energy and money into this. But what happens if an affiliate doesn't really give much value to your brand, and are just using it to make some cash? This could be dangerous as the affiliate might tarnish your reputation by misrepresenting what your brand is all about.

Present And Past Problems

From the time affiliate marketing was born, it's been difficult to control how the affiliates work. Spam has always been an issue, as has false advertising and adware. There are rules in place, but it hasn't stopped spurious affiliates from taking advantage of the system.

Email Spam

Affiliate marketing received a bad reputation early on, thanks largely to unscrupulous tactics used by affiliates who were just looking to make a quick buck before they were caught. Email spam has been a long-standing problem, but it has been reduced drastically by affiliate programs that clearly stipulate spam will not be tolerated.

Search Engine Spam

Spamming via search engines has always been a problem, too. Basically, an underhanded tactic by unethical affiliates is to make a webpage that is generated automatically. These pages usually are full of product data feed and the whole idea behind them is to alter how relevant or prominent a resource that is indexed by Google actually is.

Customer Countermeasures

Affiliate marketers must rely on various methods that are built into web designs and web pages if they are to be successful.

They also use calls that are sent out to external domains. This is so user actions are tracked, while ads are accessible by the user. All of this takes time, while casual Internet users would say this is just basically visual clutter. Countermeasures have been setup to prevent ads popping up when a web page is still being rendered. You yourself can use any number of 3rd party programs, including Ad Ware and AdBlock Plus to block unwanted ads.

Adware

Adware is different from spyware, but both use the same methods and tech. A few years ago, affiliate marketers and businesses didn't have as much information as we do now regarding adware and its effect on the customer experience, as well as the brand itself.

It was actually affiliate marketers who came along and pointed out the problem. They were savvy enough to spot that adware overwrites tracking cookies, and consequently reduces commissions. Affiliates not reliant on adware saw this as stealing their commissions. Moreover, adware doesn't really benefit anyone - especially not the user.

Affiliates then took to online forums to discuss the issue of adware and attempt to come up with a few solutions. They got organized and requested merchants that they no longer employ adware. Any merchant who didn't listen or comply was exposed and their reputations were tarnished. Indeed, these merchants eventually became blacklisted - affiliates refused to work with them.

Over time, merchants and affiliates got together to put the pressure on all affiliate programs to put an end to adware as a means of advertising. A Code of Conduct came into being. As of 2016, however, adware has not been totally eradicated. It remains an issue.

Bidding for Trademark

Back at the end of the nineties, when pay-per-click engines were new, many PPC advertisers were affiliates.

Google Adwords launched at the start of the new millennium. It's a PPC service that started the PPC "revolution" and is basically the prime reason why PPC remains so popular even today. As lots of merchants used PPC advertising, either directly or via an agency, they came across affiliates who had got there first. This caused conflict between the merchants and affiliates. One of the most seemingly insurmountable issues was that affiliates were bidding for trademarks, brands and names. Advertisers were including in their programs terms which would prevent affiliates from bidding on certain keywords.

There were exceptions, of course, and advertisers are still around who both encourage affiliates to bid on trade markers, as well as tolerate it.

Disclosure of Compensation

Disclosure guidelines have been created by the FTC which bloggers might not even be aware of. The guidelines, though, have a direct impact on the language that can be used in endorsements, ads, and compensation.

Training and Certification

There are zero industry standards when it comes to certification and training in affiliate marketing. You can get a certification from a seminar or course, but they are only begrudgingly accepted based on the reputation of the individual or school. Unfortunately, there aren't many college instructors who are actively educating their students regarding this matter.

Instead, people are left to learn about this in actual life - learning as they go. There are books available on the subject, but you can't rely on them all. Moreover, there are some books that encourage individuals to engage in underhanded tactics to gain the upper hand. For example, they recommend methods that are forbidden by affiliate networks themselves.

Code of Conduct

A Code of Conduct was set up at the end of 2002 by a few affiliate networks that was designed to safeguard the experience of affiliate marketers, as well as uphold standards.

Vulnerability To Sales Tax

In 2008, the State of New York overrode Amazon.com and ordered them to pay more tax by slotting a product into New York's budget with the rationale that certain websites in the states were linked to Amazon by affiliates.

New York argued that Amazon is basically a business in New York even if there is only one link. As such, the state had the right to tax any sale made by Amazon to the people of New York. Amazon challenged it, but lost.

CONCLUSION

Thank you for reading this book. I hope you enjoyed it and got a lot out of it, including a new sharp perspective regarding what this type of online marketing actually is, and what you need to do to make some ground in this field.

Throughout the book, I covered affiliate marketing in detail. I discussed its origins, as well as what you need to do to get started. I also covered strategies, as well as mistakes you need to avoid if you are to be successful.

Hopefully, you're now ready to make a start. My last piece of advice is that you keep checking blogs related to the field of affiliate marketing, as new techniques, strategies and trends are popping up all the time.

Good luck!

THANKS FOR READING

We really hope you enjoyed this book. If you found this material helpful feel free to share it with a friend. You can also help others find it by leaving a positive review where you purchased the book.

The Smart Reads library is growing by the day! Make sure and check out the other wonderful books we have in our catalog and let us know which ones are your favorites.

Visit:

www.smartreads.co/freebooks

to receive Smart Reads books for FREE

Check us out on Instagram:

www.instagram.com/smart_readers

@smart_readers

Don't forget your 3 FREE audiobooks. Use this link www.audibletrial.com/Travis to signup for a FREE audible account and then email me at Hello@SmartReads.co and let me know which other two books you want and I will send you credits to download the books for free!

WHY I STARTED SMART READS

I started smart reads because every time I want to learn about something new I'd have to buy 20 books on the topic and spend way too long sorting through them and reading them all until I can arrive at the big picture. Until I had enough perspectives to know who was just guessing, who was uninformed and who had stumbled upon something remarkable.

I wished someone else could just go in and figure that out for me and tell me what matters. That's how Smart Reads was born. I want Smart Reads to be a company that does all that research up front. Sorts through all the content that is available on each topic and pulls out the most up to date complete understanding. Then have people smarter than me package the best wisdom in an easy to understand way in the least amount of words possible.

For example, I got a new puppy so I wanted to learn about dog training. I bought 14 different books about dog training and by the time I got through the first 5 and finally started seeing the big picture on the best way to train my puppy, she had grown up into a dog.

Yeah she's well behaved. She doesn't poop in the house. I can get her to sit and come when I call. But what if someone else went in and read all those books for me. Found the underlying themes and picked out the best information that would give me the big picture and get me right to the point. And I'd only have to read one book instead of 15. That would be amazing. I would save time. And maybe my dog would be rolling over, cleaning up after my kid and doing the dishes by now.

That my friends, is the reason I started smart reads. Because I wanted a company I can trust to deliver me the best information in an easy to understand way that I can digest quickly. Because dog training is one of many subjects I want to master and bring into the rest of my life. And the quicker I can learn a wide variety of topics the sooner that information can begin playing a role in shaping my future. And none of us knows how long that future will be. So why not do everything we can to make the best of it.

WE WANT TO HELP PLANT A BILLION TREES

For every 10 hardcover books we sell we are going to plant a tree in collaboration with www.plantabillion.org to make up for the paper we use printing the books and to do our part helping to regain our valuable forests.

SMART READS ORIGINS

Smart Reads was born out of the desire to find the best information fast without having to wade through the sheer volume of fluff available for purchase. Smart Reads combs through massive amounts of knowledge accessible online and compiles all the best into easily digestible books on a wide variety of subjects.

We consider ourselves Smart Readers, not dummies. We like to learn a TON about a WIDE variety of topics. It's the best way to capture the big picture! With the amount of noise in the marketplace today, each new topic we try to learn about begins with a never ending search to find facts that matter. It becomes a treasure hunt rather than an education.

Smart Reads aims to be your one-stop-shop for superior information on any subject you want to learn about. When you see a Smart Reads book on your topic of interest you know your search for quality information is over. As a smart reader, you get more information on more topics in less time.

OUR MISSION

Smart Reads mission is to accelerate the spread and availability of valuable information. We believe having access to knowledge is a basic human right and want to see every person on the planet be able to learn about any topic that would enhance their lives. We hope to remove barriers to sharing by taking the copyright off everything we publish and donating it to the public domain.

We also know we can't accomplish this mission by ourselves so we are giving 5% of our net profit to Pencils of Promise. We hope to donate $1,000,000 or more by 2020 to build over 2,000 schools and increase educational opportunities in the developing world.

By purchasing from Smart Reads you are contributing to helping kids all over the globe get access to a valuable education they otherwise wouldn't have had.

Doesn't it feel good knowing that by educating yourself you are helping to educate the next generation? We think so too…

Thanks for choosing Smart Reads! You Smart Reader you…

Travis and the Smart Reads Team

Customers Who Bought This Book Also Bought

Success Principles: Techniques for Positive Thinking, Self-Love and Developing a Powerful Mindset

Artificial Intelligence: Understanding A.I. and the Implications of Machine Learning

Credit Repair Guide: How to Fix Credit Score and Remove Negatives From Credit Report

Develop Self-Discipline: Daily Habit to Make Self Confidence and Will Power Automatic

How To Control Alcoholism: Proven Techniques
to Stop Alcohol Abuse, Overcome Dependency,
Break Addiction and Recover Your Life

Self-Esteem Supercharger: Build Self Worth and
Find Your Inner Confidence

Dealing with Anxiety: Modern Techniques for an
Age Old Condition